The Great Depression – A Short History

By Doug West, Ph.D.

The Great Depression – A Short History

Copyright © 2016 Doug West

Table of Contents

Preface

Welcome to the book *The Great Depression – A Short History*. This book is part of the "30 Minute Book Series" and, as the name of the series implies, if you are an average reader this book will take around 30 minutes to read. Since this book is not meant to be an all-encompassing story of The Great Depression, you may want to know more about this terrible time in America and the world. To help you with this, there are several good references at the end of this book. Thank you for purchasing this book and I hope you enjoy your time reading about this tumultuous period in history.

Doug West

February 2016

Introduction

The Great Depression, like most other periods of severe unemployment, was produced by government mismanagement rather than by any inherent instability of the private economy. - Milton Friedman

There are many theories as to why the United States and then much of the world entered into a long period of price deflation, high unemployment, and an overall significant economic downturn, which we now call the Great Depression. People always wonder why this horrendous event occurred and there is no simple answer to this question. It was a perfect storm of events that came together and brought about an inevitable plummet in the lives of millions. Perhaps the opening shot of this dark period was the stock market crash in October of 1929. Nothing had happened like it before that moment. In the aftermath, the rest of the country and the world fell into the Great Depression, the longest and deepest economic depression since the Civil War.

During the 1920s, the United States economy was growing and the stock market kept reaching new highs. Lot of common people were making money in the stock market and having a grand time; unfortunately, there were ominous clouds few noticed on the horizon. By that time, industrial production had started declining and unemployment was already rising. The signs were there, but many were ignored. Some of the causes of the collapse were the explosion of debt, low wages, an agricultural industry that was struggling, and large bank loans that were unable to be liquidated.

Prices started to decline from the stock market peak in September of 1929, and on October 18, the market began to fall dramatically. Panic began to set in with the traders and investors, and on October 24, known as "Black Thursday," the market lost 11 percent of its value on the opening bell in heavy trading. Investment companies and bankers tried to stabilize the market through purchasing blocks of stock, producing a moderate improvement by Friday. However, by Monday, the market was in trouble once again. On October 29, over sixteen million shares were traded in just one day. Billions of dollars had been lost, thousands of investors had been wiped out, and stock tickers were running hours behind because the machinery couldn't handle the unprecedented amount of trading.

After October 29, the stock prices should have gone up; however, prices overall kept dropping as the United States fell into the Great Depression, and by the time 1932 came around, stocks were worth just twenty percent of what they had previously been worth in 1929. The crash was not the only cause of the Great Depression; it was more of a symptom of a larger set of problems.

Earlier in 1929, Herbert Hoover had won the presidency under a wealth and prosperity platform. Hoover made unsuccessful attempts to prevent the economy from worsening during his administration, banks continued to fail, and more Americans entered the ranks of the unemployed. No one really understood just how far the economy had to fall. By 1933, hundreds of the United States' banks had gone under, and unemployment rapidly approached fifteen million people, which was roughly thirty percent of the working age population.

The election of 1932 brought the Democrat, Franklin D. Roosevelt, into the office of the President by a landslide. The American people wanted change for the better and quickly too. Roosevelt wasted no time and proposed a plethora of legislation that was called the New Deal. The New Deal programs were designed to put people back to work, stop the bank failures, and give hope to the people. Some of the New Deal programs were successful, while other were not, but by the end of the 1930s, things were starting to improve. It would take the massive spending required for America's role in World War II before the economy would rebound to where it had been over a decade before.

CHAPTER 1

The Roaring Twenties

I have no fears for the future of the country. It is bright with hope. – Herbert Hoover

The Jazz Age, the Roaring Twenties, or simply, the 1920s, was a period of rapid expansion in the economy. Social attitudes were shifting and society was starting to be less regimented. People were exploring new freedoms, and their expectations were changing too. These changes were powered by the growing economy and the introduction of many new technologies — automobiles, tractors, electricity, radio, telephones. However, behind this seemingly robust economy and the optimistic views were some serious structural problems, which would be manifest in the stock market crash of 1929.

In the 1920s, economic growth was unusually high, leading to a significant increase in living standards. The reasons behind this economic growth were the growing automobile industry, increased consumer confidence, technology improvements, labor productivity improvements, mass production, and the laissez-faire government attitude toward business. The government had virtually a "hands off" approach to business. Republicans were in the White House and they favored lower taxes, especially for the higher income tax brackets. In 1925,

President Calvin Coolidge spoke before the American Society of Newspaper Editors and told the crowd: "After all, the chief business of the American people is business. They are profoundly concerned with producing, buying, selling, investing, and prospering in the world."

During this period, anti-trust laws were slackened, allowing the growth of monopoly businesses, such as banking. Union memberships declined as the government offered very little legal support for unions. One of the largest names in the car manufacturing business, Henry Ford, banned trade unions at his factories. However, Ford paid wages that were much higher than anywhere else, so his workers never seemed to mind the lack of a union.

With this boost in the economy also came a growth in personal debt as individuals began using credit rather than cash, and this attitude extended into the stock market as well. No longer was the stock market the playground of the wealthy; now the common man with a few extra dollars could invest in a company through the purchase of stock. To fuel the speculative frenzy, the stockbrokers lent money to their clients, called margin, to allow them to purchase even more stock. As the stock market kept rising, it seemed like a safe and easy way to make money, which encouraged more speculators to take the risk. Unfortunately, share prices seemed to be based on anything but the fundamentals of the business.

Figure – Family in a Model T Ford circa 1920

The boom during the 1920s did not extend to every sector of the economy, being mainly focused on car manufacturing and the construction industry. During most of the twenties, the agricultural sector fought to stay afloat due to declining prices. Farmers became more productive with the use of the gas-powered tractor, a machine that revolutionized the farming industry. Farmers who bought tractors were able to grow their crops at a lower cost because they were able to farm more fields, and those who did not embrace the new technologies began to fall behind. The farmers who were not able to keep up with their well-equipped peers started to go out of business and leave the farm, leading to a shift in population from rural areas to urban areas.

In addition to these population changes and the struggling agricultural sector, there was structural weakness within the small and medium-sized banks. This meant that when the Great Depression did hit, the banking sector wasn't prepared to face the terrible circumstances. Even before the depression took hold, many regional banks were quietly facing problems. The smaller banks were poorly capitalized and when a large farming operation went bankrupt, the bank holding the loan was thrown into financial turmoil.

The roaring twenties were full of people who were living on credit, borrowing more than they could pay back; banks who were lending out money at high rates; and a stock market that was operating outside of the bounds of reality — this would all soon change.

CHAPTER 2

The 1929 Stock Market Crash

*After 1929, so many people had been traumatized by the
stock market crash that there was a lost generation.*
- Ron Chernow

Most of the stock market crash could be blamed on the false
expectations of the investors and businesses alike, and the in-
flated excitement levels. In the years that led up to 1929, the
stock market was offering the potential for many people to
make huge gains in wealth — it was the new gold rush. The
stock market had been on a nine-year climb that saw the Dow
Jones Industrial Average increase tenfold, peaking at 381 on
September 3, 1929.

People purchased shares with the expectation that they'd
make money. As more people became buyers, the share prices
increased. To make even more profit, speculators began to
borrow money to invest. The market became caught up in this
huge, speculative bubble. Shares continued to rise and people felt they would continue to keep going up. The problem
was that the stock prices were separated from the reality-ba-
sed earnings of the companies. Prices were not driven by the
economic fundamentals, but by the increasing number of new,
optimistic investors.

Stocks were being purchased on the margin, allowing customers to pay only ten to twenty percent of the value of the shares up front and borrowing eighty to ninety percent of the value of the shares from the broker. This allowed more money to be put into the shares, which increased their values. Investors made large profits through purchasing on margin and watching the share prices rise. However, this left investors exposed when the prices dropped. These "margin millionaires" were wiped out when the stock market fell and the broker demanded more money to cover the increasing margin requirements. It also affected the brokers and banks who'd lent the money to those who bought on margin.

In March of 1929, the stock market saw the first major reversal. This mini-panic was suppressed by a strong rebound in the summer of the same year. However, by October, the shares were hugely overvalued and when some companies posted disappointing results for their profits, many investors felt it was a good time to cash in on their pricey shares. The crash had begun.

By the middle of 1929, there were many, including the Federal Reserve Board and several Senators, who felt the price of equity securities had skyrocketed past reality. This belief was reinforced on a daily basis by the media and statements that were made by influential government officials.

On Wednesday, October 16, 1929, the stock prices started to decline again. The *Washington Post's* headline on the front page was "Crushing Blow Again Dealt Stock Market." The news reports from the *Washington Post* on October 17 and the following days were important because they were Associated Press releases, meaning they were readily available throughout the entire country.

On Wednesday, October 23, the market plummeted. The *New York Times* reported "Prices of Stocks Crash in Heavy Liquidation" and the *Washington Post* reported "Huge Selling Wave Creates Near-Panic as Stocks Collapse." In a market valued at eighty-seven billion dollars, four billion dollars were lost. It was almost a five percent drop. If the events that occurred on the following day had not happened, October 23 would have been considered Black Wednesday, but it was merely a dip compared to the next twenty-four hours.

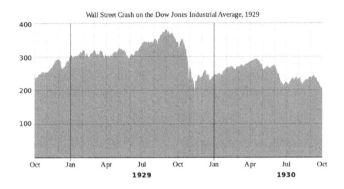

Wall Street Crash on the Dow Jones Industrial Average, 1929

Figure – 1929 Stock Market Chart

On October 24, 1929, "Black Thursday," the market lost 11 percent of its value at the start of trading on heavy volume. The number of shares trading hands was so large that the ticker tape machines were hours behind in printing out all the transactions from the day, and this left investors not knowing exactly what they sold their shares for until hours later. Several Wall Street bankers had an emergency meeting to find a solution to the chaos and panic that had gripped the trading floor. The bankers purchased large numbers of shares of "blue chip" stock, which helped support the market. This succeeded in slowing the panic selling and the market closed down six points for the day. The *Wall Street Journal* released an article giving the New York bankers credit for stopping the price decline with one billion dollars of support.

On Monday, October 28, more investors facing margin calls decided to get out of the market and sell their shares. The Dow suffered a record loss of 13 percent that day. The selling continued the next day, "Black Tuesday," as the Dow Jones Industrial Average lost an additional 30 points, or 12 percent. The volume of stocks traded that day would set a record that would take nearly four decades to eclipse. The stocks lost almost sixteen billion dollars in the month of October. Twenty-nine public utilities had lost over five billion dollars that month.

Over the next several years, the stock market rallied and suffered setbacks repeatedly. The bottom of the market did not come until July 8, 1932, when the Dow closed at 41 — the lowest level of the twentieth century. The Dow Jones Industrial Average would not surpass the September high of 1929 until 1954.

Though less than one-in-five Americans owned stocks and suffered directly from the crash, the psychological effects of the crash reverberated throughout the nation. The crash had a chilling effect on businesses, making it harder for them to secure capital market investments for new projects and expansion. Thus, the downward spiral had begun. The uncertainty within the business community naturally affected the job security of the employees. The workers, unsure of their next paycheck, cut back on spending, which lowered the demand for consumer products. It was a vicious cycle that would take years to run its course.

CHAPTER 3

The Hoover Administration's Response

Economic depression cannot be cured by legislative action or executive pronouncement. Economic wounds must be healed by the action of the cells of the economic body — the producers and consumers themselves. - Herbert Hoover

President Herbert Hoover is forever associated with the opening act of the depression as he came into office in March of 1929. By then, the stock market and the economy were starting to show signs of weakness. Through the rearview mirror of history, we see that Hoover's response to the growing problem was too little to be effective. The problem with the economy was a much larger problem than nearly anyone imagined.

Hoover started his presidency with a burst of enthusiasm and energy that showcased his progressive political viewpoints. He instructed the Department of the Interior to improve conditions for the Native Americans on the reservations which were controlled by the government. He managed to pass the Boulder Canyon Project Act, an act that allowed the construction of the massive dam later named after the President himself. This dam provided power for the public utilities in California. He also appointed Horace Albright to the National

Park Service and put nearly two million acres of federal land into a national forest reserve to conserve natural resources.

There were two issues that took center stage during his first nine months as president: improving the economic health of the agricultural sector and tax reform. When he entered office, he called Congress into a special session to address these problems.

Figure – President Hebert Hoover

Farmers suffered during the 1920s as their incomes shrank to only a third of the national average. The chief problem was overproduction. They benefited from the new technologies that increased their productivity, which had the effect of causing over-production of their products. And this, along with competition from overseas, caused the prices at the market to drop dramatically. Many were demanding federal government subsidies to boost their farm's incomes. The President and his Congressional allies both opposed subsidies; instead, he supported a bill that made the Federal Farm Board. With a five million-dollar budget, the farm board loaned money to farmers to make and strengthen farm cooperatives in the hope that they would control production and bring the crops to market in a more efficient manner. There was a political deadlock that persisted and factions of Congress battled over the farm policy. Hoover did little to calm this uproar.

In June of 1929, Congress passed the Agricultural Marketing Act, complete with the Federal Farm Board and no subsidies. Hoover obtained his agricultural program but not without a significant cost politically. By the fall of 1929, the board was up and running.

Tax policies, the other early challenge Hoover faced, had been a flashpoint in American politics. In his State of the Union message, delivered December 3, Hoover stressed the positive effects that a tax cut would have on the nation. "We cannot fail to recognize the obligations of the government in support of the public welfare," he declared, "but we must coincidentally bear in mind the burden of taxes and strive to find relief through some tax reduction. Every dollar so returned fertilizes the soil of prosperity." Inside the Capitol, the tax reduction plan was well received. Republicans were openly supportive and even a few Democrats endorsed the plan. Hoover's tax cut plan was passed by both houses without major changes. Unfortunately, the small tax cuts once in place had no discernible effect on the course of the economy.

The stock market's collapse and the Great Depression didn't catch Hoover completely off-guard, but, like most Americans, he was shocked by the severity of the developments. Prior to his term as President, as the Secretary of Commerce, he worried about the speculation in the stock market and even asked for government regulation of banks and stock exchanges to prevent insider trading and margin buying. He also proposed that the Federal Reserve Board raise the interest rates, but the board lowered them, thus fueling the stock market boom that occurred in the two years leading up to his presidency.

During the first few months of his presidency, Hoover and key advisors all voiced their concerns about the future and shape of the economy. He supported the Agricultural Marketing Act because he thought this would protect the weaker sector. Suspicious of the stock speculation, he approved the efforts by the Federal Reserve System to convince the New York Federal Reserve Bank to stop the practice of discounts to smaller banks, a practice that many believe fueled the stock market speculation. Hoover was uncertain of the wisdom of the Federal Reserve Board asking the member banks to tighten the money supply in order to stop the speculative loans.

During the peak selling of the stock market crash in October of 1929, Hoover reacted by stating that, "The fundamental business of the country, that is production and distribution of commodities, is on a sound and prosperous basis." Behind the scenes, however, he and the administration worked hard to counter what they thought might be the beginning of an economic downturn. His advisors made proposals to stimulate the economy by reducing taxes, loosening credit policies at the Federal Reserve level, and spending on public works. He also called openly for the state and local governments to expand their public works projects. In November of 1929, he organized several conferences that brought the leaders of the labor, industry, and government together to discuss the economy. He asked for and received pledges from the industry sector to not cut jobs or wages, and from the labor unions to not press for higher wages.

His actions in the wake of the stock market crash were based on his belief that the economy faced a downturn rather than a nearly complete collapse. He urged the cooperation amongst the industry and labor sectors. He ordered the Department of Labor and Commerce to come up with a precise and accurate economic statistics report. Unfortunately for him, the report showed that in the week and a half before Christmas of 1929, one million Americans had lost their jobs.

To make matters worse, in June of 1930, Congress passed the Smoot-Hawley Tariff, which was supported by Hoover. The mis-guided attempt to boost farm income greatly increased the tariff on agricultural raw materials and other products. These high rates, which were meant to protect domestic industry, made it difficult for other countries to trade with the United States. The reduction in trade hurt both the United States and their trading partners, and contributed to the spread of the depression throughout the world.

Hoover continued to struggle throughout the remainder of 1930 and 1931. He called for more federal assistance and justified it by stating that the country used emergency powers in order to win a war so they could use them to battle the Great Depression. Unfortunately, none of these approaches were especially effective.

Figure – Crowd at New York's American Union Bank during a run on the bank.

By the fall of 1930, waves of banking panics gripped the United States. A run on a bank would occur when nervous depositors lost confidence in the bank and demanded their money back in cash. Banks held only a fraction of their deposits in cash reserves, so as the demand for cash became too large, they would attempt to liquidate loans to raise cash. This process of hasty liquidation of loans resulted in the banks receiving less than full value for the loan and caused many banks to fail. Before the end of the depression, thousands of banks failed, forcing thousands of bank employees to look for work elsewhere.

In 1931, Hoover urged bankers to set up the National Credit Corporation so large banks could help small banks survive. The National Credit Corporation was short-lived due to its private-sector leaders that were not accommodating and refused to bail out the smaller banks. As this corporation failed, the Hoover administration created the Reconstruction Finance Corporation. In 1932, this was supposed to be government run and funded and was meant to stabilize the financial structure of the nation through providing credit to banks that were both weak and strong, as well as other entities like agricultural organizations and railroad construction. The President hoped that by improving the financial health of the nation, public confidence would be boosted and employment opportunities and international trade would grow. While they often failed to help out the smaller banks, just as the National Credit Corporation, economists and historians sing its praise for saving many of the larger financial institutions from going under. However, the Reconstruction Finance Corporation didn't fulfill Hoover's hopes of cutting down on unemployment.

The effects of the downturn had left hundreds of thousands of Americans homeless and they began to congregate in shantytowns — dubbed "Hoovervilles" — which started to appear in cities all over the country. To help with the growing numbers of homeless and unemployed, in the summer of 1932, Hoover enacted the Emergency Relief Construction Act. This provided two billion dollars to public works projects and three hundred million dollars for direct relief programs that were run by the state governments. While the bill was only a pittance of direct relief and put many restrictions on how that three hundred million dollars could be used, the endorsement by Hoover testified to the failure of private relief and voluntarism. Hoover saw this as a temporary measure to provide some emergency relief and remained opposed to large-scale and permanent government costs on relief and welfare programs.

In March of 1932, Hoover approved the Norris-La Guardia Act or, as it was also known, the Anti-Injunction Bill. This accomplished three objectives that were supported by labor unions. First, it restricted the use of yellow-dog contracts where employers hired replacement workers in order to break a strike. Second, it made it very difficult for federal judges to issue a sweeping injunction against strikes. And finally, it confirmed the rights of laborers to organize. It was an important forerunner of the 1935 Wagner Act.

To pay the programs and increase federal revenue, Congress passed the Revenue Act of 1932, which was the largest peace-time tax increase in history. The Act increased taxes to the point where the top earners were paying 63% of their income in taxes. The Act also raised corporate taxes but to a lesser extent. In addition to the Revenue Act of 1932, Hoover also agreed to remove several tax cuts that his Administration had enacted to benefit the upper income individual. The estate tax was doubled and a "check tax" was introduced that placed a two-cent tax on all bank checks. Looking back, economists today view these new taxes as making a significant contribution to the detrimental contraction of the money supply during the depression.

CHAPTER 4

Bonus Army March on Washington, D.C.

You are remembered for the rules you break.
- General Douglas MacArthur

Perhaps the saddest chapter of the Great Depression occurred in 1932, when tens of thousands of unemployed American World War I veterans marched into Washington, D.C. to demand the bonuses owed them for their service in the war, and were forced out of the city at the point of a gun. After World War I, veterans lobbied Congress for back compensation for their earnings lost as a result of their service in the military. In 1924, the government agreed to compensate the veterans at approximately one dollar per day that they served during the war; however, the payment wasn't due until 1945. A bill was put forth in the House of Representatives in 1932 to pay the veterans at that time in order to help alleviate their suffering brought on by the depression. Once word of the impending legislation was out, tens of thousands of veterans from all over the country descended on Washington, D.C. to lobby for passage of the "bonus" bill, as it would be known. The loosely organized group of marchers dubbed themselves the Bonus Expeditionary Force or BFE, whose name was a play on the World War I American Expeditionary Forces. The media called the group the "Bonus March."

The practice of war-time military bonuses began with the Revolutionary War, as a payment for the difference between what a soldier earned and what he could have earned if not in the military. Breaking with tradition, veterans of the Spanish-American War did not receive a bonus, and after World War I the veterans only received a meager $60 bonus. The American legion, which was established in 1919, led a political movement for an additional bonus.

Hoover, though against the idea of the accelerated payments of the bonuses, provided the marchers with food and shelter, supporting their right to demonstrate. While they were in Washington, some of the veterans and their families took up temporary residence in buildings that were scheduled to be demolished. After the Senate voted down the bonus legislation, most of the veterans left Washington and went home. Some remained in the abandoned buildings and in camps along the river. Most of the marchers camped in a Hooverville on the Anacostia Flats, a swampy area across the Anacostia River from the federal core of Washington. After the debate was over, Congress and Hoover both agreed that the remaining demonstrators needed to be disbursed. Hoover gave strict instructions for a peaceful disbursement carried out by the existing army, but it didn't go according to plan.

Patrick Hurley, the Secretary of War, feared the demonstrators might riot and exceeded the President's instructions and ordered General Douglas MacArthur to relocate the marchers. The General exceeded his orders and drove the demonstrators, using force, from Washington, D.C. The Army and police attacked the veterans and their families using tear gas, tanks, guns, and bayonets, and they burned the camps along the river. Two demonstrators were killed and dozens of others were seriously injured during the Army's destruction of their shantytowns. MacArthur's treatment of the Bonus Army shocked and disappointed Colonel Dwight Eisenhower, one of his aides, who later recalled it as, "A pitiful scene, those ragged, discouraged people burning their own little things."

Figure – Bonus Army Camp being burnt at Anacostia Flats.

By the time news of the excessive force used by the military reached the newspapers, Hoover's bid for re-election was defeated before it even had a chance. MacArthur refused to take responsibility, as did his superiors, leaving President Hoover to take responsibility for orders he never administered. Images of the attack and the rampage were all over the newspaper, and the president's standing with the public tanked.

A second Bonus March occurred in 1933 at the start of the Roosevelt administration, but this one was diffused with offers of jobs in the Civilian Conservation Corps, or CCC, at Fort Hunt, Virginia. Those marchers not wanting to work for the CCC were provided transportation back home. In 1936, Congress overrode President Roosevelt's veto and paid the veterans their bonuses nine years early.

CHAPTER 5

President Roosevelt and the New Deal

The only thing we have to fear is fear itself.
- Franklin D. Roosevelt

The presidential election of 1932 was America's reaction to the adversity imposed by the Great Depression. The anger and frustration of the people forced the Republican Party and Herbert Hoover out of power and, in their place, the Democrat Franklin Delano Roosevelt took office. The election was a landslide for Roosevelt, wining 42 states and a popular majority of nearly seven million votes. In his inaugural address, Roosevelt promised "A New Deal for the American people" and stated, "This nation asks for action, and action now."

President Roosevelt wasted no time as he quickly called for a national "banking holiday," which closed all banks and allowed only certain banks to re-open once they had been deemed solvent by government inspectors. Roosevelt called for a special session of Congress and they quickly passed the Emergency Banking Act to provide help to the banks. By 1933, one-fifth of the banks that were in existence when Herbert Hoover took office had failed.

In a legislative frenzy known as "One Hundred Days," Roosevelt and Congress passed many new pieces of legislation to help restore the country to financial health. Over the next several years, Roosevelt, through the New Deal policies, greatly expanded the role of government in the lives of the average American. The New Deal began a political realignment that positioned the Democratic Party as the new majority. This party based their platform on liberal beliefs, empowering labor unions, minorities, and the white South. There were some Republicans who supported this program, while most of them were non-supportive and claimed these programs were destructive to business and development.

Relief was geared toward helping those who were unemployed find employment and those who were poor find a way to survive. Unemployment during the Great Depression was running rampant. At the depth of the depression in 1933, twenty-five percent of the American population was unable to find employment, which meant there were more than thirteen million people unemployed. Factory orders were down and the low production had led to major layoffs of workers. The jobless had very little money left to spend and businesses began to gradually fail. More and more Americans relied on the government dole in order to feed their families.

The CCC, or Civilian Conservation Corps, was a New Deal program set up to provide employment for young unmarried men between the ages of 17 and 28. The program had a long run from 1933 to 1942 and was one of the most popular programs, with three million young men participating in it. The CCC provided the men with shelter, clothing, food, and a small wage of $30 per month, of which $25 had to be sent home to their families. The program was responsible for planting billions of trees to help reforest America, constructed hundreds of parks nationwide, and built a network of service buildings and public roadways.

Figure – CCC Recruitment Poster form 1935

Another program to spur employment was the PWA or Public Works Administration. The organization built large-scale public works projects, such as, dams, bridges, hospitals, and schools. Over the life of the program from 1933 to 1943, six billion dollars were put into contracts to private construction firms that did the actual labor.

Farmers were a group that was especially hard hit by the depression. The lower commodity prices resulted in large numbers of farms failing. To compound the plight of the farmers, the 1930s saw a significant drought which, when combined with the deep plowing of the top soil of the Great Plains allowed by the gasoline tractors, produced large scale wind erosion of the soil. As the ground baked in the hot sun and the wind blew, the exposed soil became fine dust particles and, becoming airborne, they produced large dust storms that moved across vast areas. The enormous dust storms made the sky black, and as the dust fell from the sky the land was covered with the fine dust, causing problems for those in the path of the dust storms. Texas, Oklahoma, and the adjacent states saw the most impact of the storms on their agricultural industry, resulting in millions of people migrating out of these states looking for work in the Western states like California.

Figure – Dust Storm in Texas circa 1935

Some measures created to help the farmers who were trying to survive were the AAA or Agricultural Adjustment Act, Commodity Credit Corporation, and Soil Conservation Service. The AAA was meant to give economic aid to farmers who were paid to keep land out of production and thus reduce the available crops for sale. The Commodity Credit Corporation bought goods to store them until the prices rose. The Soil Conservation Service was an agency created by the government to provide relief to farmers to help them prevent soil erosion and implement improved farming techniques.

The first New Deal was deemed inadequate and the government and the private sector decided to move on to the Second New Deal. This new round of legislation, enacted in 1935, was a compilation of laws focused on the goal of economic security. In his address to Congress in January of 1935, President Roosevelt called for: improved use of national resources; security for the elderly, ill, and unemployed; slum clearance; and a national welfare program to replace the existing state programs. Some of the most important programs that came of the second New Deal included Social Security, rural electrification, and the Banking Act of 1935. Liberals strongly supported the new direction and formed the New Deal Coalition of union members, big city political machines, the white South, and ethnic minorities. Conservatives strongly opposed the legislation as an over-reach of government and an impediment to business.

The National Labor Relations Act, which was often called the Wagner Act, placed the authority of the federal government behind the labor unions and collective bargaining. If the majority of the company's workers wanted a union, management was required to cooperate with the organization of a union. The Wagner Act rejuvenated organized labor and many important industries became unionized. A National Labor Relations Board was established to enforce the legislation.

In 1936, President Roosevelt was elected a second time. He took sixty-percent of the votes and was able to form a new coalition with the Democratic Party that reached farmers, laborers, urbanites, and minorities in the North and South. He was supported by the middle-class citizens and businesses from towns and suburbs, and his formidable alliance that stood for decades.

The New Deal policies were not without controversy and several of the programs were challenged in the court system. In 1936, the Agricultural Administration Act and the National Recovery Administration were invalidated by the Supreme Court as unconstitutional over-extensions of the government. New incarnations of the agencies, which passed the tests of the court system, emerged over the next few years.

During his presidency, there was a large debate as to whether or not the New Deal policies would boost the economy and improve people's lives. The citizens wished for a government that would assume responsibility for the welfare of the ordinary person. The New Deal did lay down the foundation for the welfare state in the United States and increased regulations of business and industry.

Despite his best efforts, it wasn't until World War II came along that the Great Depression finally ended. During the period from 1929 to 1939, the percent of the growth domestic product of nonmilitary spending of the federal government had grown from 1.5 percent to 7.5 percent. However comprehensive the New Deal seemed, it failed in its main goal to end the depression. In 1939, the unemployment rate was still high at 19 percent, and it would not be until 1943 before the unemployment rate would return to its pre-depression level. A much larger federal government is one of the legacies of the Great Depression that is still in effect today.

CHAPTER 6

International Effects of the Great Depression

*True individual freedom cannot exist without economic secu-
rity and independence. People who are hungry and out of a
job are the stuff of which dictatorships are made.*
- Franklin D. Roosevelt

Whether the depression started in the United States and spread
like a contagion to other parts of the world, or whether there were many nations with weak economic fundamentals and
America was the first to fall, is an on-going debate among
historians and economists. Whatever the cause-and-effect re-
lationship, the United States was not the only nation to suffer
economically during the 1930s.

The economic downturn in North America and Europe had
a serious impact on Third World countries that were heavily
dependent on exports. As the export markets for these countries dried up, so did the flow of investment dollars from the
United States. Many countries, especially in Latin America,
responded by introducing high tariffs and attempting to beco-
me more self-sufficient.

The United States' northern neighbor, Canada, was especially
hard hit by the economic slowdown. At the time, the Canadian
economy was starting to transition from an economy based

on primary industries, such as farming, fishing, mining, and logging, to a more modern industrial economy. As the demand for their export products fell, so did the prices for those products. Between 1929 and 1939, prices dropped by 40% and unemployment reached 27% during the depths of the depression in 1933.

Like much of the world, Canada's economy emerged from the depression with the outbreak of World War II. With the growing conflict in Europe came an increased demand for Canadian exports. Unemployed men were able to enlist in the military and the Canadian government increased spending to boost the economy. By 1939, Canada was beginning to experience a period of growth and relative prosperity.

Great Britain, at the start of the Great Depression, was in a different financial position than the United States, as it had recovered little from the devastation of the First World War. Britain had missed much of the prosperity experienced by Western countries in the 1920s and the global downturn in the 1930s only worsened their problems. A significant factor for Britain's slow recovery was their return to the Gold Standard in 1925, which valued the Pound Sterling at the pre-war exchange rate of $4.86 US dollars to one Pound Sterling. This made the British Pound a very expensive currency relative to other nations and hurt their export markets. To offset the effects of the high currency exchange rate, the British exporters tried to lower costs by reducing wages of the employees. Through the 1920s, unemployment remained high and by 1930, one in five workers were unemployed and exports had fallen by one half.

In 1931, the British Chancellor Philip Snowden and his administration put in place an emergency budget which cut government spending and reduced wages. This had a deflationary effect on the economy and increased the number of unemployed. Due to mounting pressure on the government, the Gold Standard was dropped and the Pound Sterling lost approximately one-quarter of its exchange value quickly. The weaker currency had the effect of increasing exports, which was the beginning of a mild recovery. The number of unemployed began to fall from 1933 onwards. As a result of the currency devaluation, interest rates were cut from 6% to 2%, which stimulated a recovery in housing construction. By 1937, the rising threat from Nazi Germany forced the government to institute a massive rebuilding of the military.

Much like Great Britain, Germany was especially hard hit by the global slowdown as it had not recovered from the First World War by the start of the 1930s. The Allied powers, in the Treaty of Versailles, demanded that Germany pay war reparations to European countries for the damage they had inflicted on the other countries during the First World War. Germany was required to pay 20 billion gold marks as an interim amount, and the final amount of the reparations would be settled at a later date. The payments were large and placed a heavy burden on the weak Germany economy. By 1923, Germany had defaulted on its required payments of money, coal, and steel. In response, French and Belgian troops occupied the Ruhr River Valley in Germany.

The German people passively resisted this occupation, which contributed to the hyperinflation that followed. The high inflation of prices in the 1920s destroyed the savings of the German people, bankrupted certain companies, and destroyed the economic foundation of the middle class. The United States stepped in to help Germany in 1924 in the form of large loans to stabilize their currency and boost the economy. The loans helped, the free-fall of the German economy was halted, and the economy slowly began to improve. The loan payments were very high and the German government struggled to make the large payments to the bank. As a result of the unrealistic payment expected, the loans were restructured as part of the Young Plan, which reduced the amount of the payments in 1930. The committee to restructure Germany's payments was headed by the American industrialist Owen D. Young, who was the creator of the Radio Corporation of America. In a bit of very bad timing, the effects of the depression were hitting America hard and US banks started recalling loans made to Europeans. The removal of the financial support threw Germany into the economic abyss.

In 1931, five of the main German banks closed as did thousands of other businesses closed. The global downturn placed many Germans out of work and forced them to seek government handouts to survive. By 1932, 40% of the workforce was unemployed.

Figure – Adolf Hitler in 1938

Even though the Young Plan had effectively reduced Germany's obligations, it was rejected by conservative groups. A coalition was formed to oppose the payment of war reparations by various conservative groups. The coalition was headed by Alfred Hugenberg, who was the head of the German National

People's Party. One of the groups that joined the coalition was Adolf Hitler and the Nationalist Socialist German Workers Party. Even though the coalition was unsuccessful in their efforts to denounce all war reparations, the movement was a major factor in bringing Hitler and the National Socialists into the political mainstream. Within days of Franklin Roosevelt becoming President in 1933, Adolf Hitler became Chancellor of Germany.

Hitler's approach to reviving the faltering German economy was in some ways similar to Roosevelt's New Deal, in that Hitler borrowed heavily to finance public works projects. By the late 1930s, Germany had reached full employment. Though Germany had emerged from the Great Depression, it was now destined to ignite World War II and throw much of the world once again into chaos.

CHAPTER 7

The Great Depression's Impact on America

My parents were children during the Great Depression of the 1930s, and it scarred them. Especially my father, who saw destitution in his Brooklyn, New York neighborhood; adults standing in so called 'bread lines,' children begging in the streets. - Bill O'Reilly

Nearly all Americans in some fashion were affected by the Great Depression. For the majority, it was a hard time and forever changed their lives. For a lucky few with steady jobs or plenty of money in the bank, as prices fell, their purchasing power actually increased. Some people even prospered during the hard times.

As the unemployment rate rose during the depression, so did the crime rate. Men and women desperate to put food on the table resorted to petty theft. The anxieties brought on by the hardships caused the suicide rate to increase significantly. Prostitution was also on the rise as desperate women sought ways to generate income. Alcoholism increased as Americans sought ways to escape, at least for a while, their dire circumstances. Cigarettes became more popular as people switched from the more expensive cigars to the less expensive alternative.

The enrollment in colleges and universities declined during the period because of the cost; however, high school attendance increased due to the lack of jobs available for the new graduates. The sharp drop in public funding hurt most schools, causing understaffing and closures.

The marriage rate declined as many males waited until they could provide for a family before they proposed to their prospective spouse. Divorce rates dropped during the 1930s, while the rate of abandonment increased. Many husbands choose the "poor man's divorce" option and simply abandoned their families. Couples weren't having as many children and the birth rate fell sharply. Contraception became more widespread as couples tried to avoid the added expense of an additional child.

The widespread use of automobiles during the 1930s allowed those facing hardship the mobility to look for work and better opportunities. Rural New England and upstate New York as well as states in the Great Plains lost population to states like California and Arizona. The lengthy drought in the 1930s sent many "okies" and "arkies" looking for a better life in the Western states. The majority of the immigrants were young men on the move in search of a better future. During the decade of the 1930s, over a half a million people were caught hitching rides on trains, many of which went unpunished.

Figure – Migrant Worker Florence Owens Thompson
taken in 1936.

One of the long term effects of the Great Depression was the increased role of the federal government in the day-to-day lives of Americans. Prior to the depression, the government had a laissez-faire approach to governing, especially regarding how businesses conducted their operations. This all changed with the trickle of new legislation introduced by the Hoover administration and then a torrent of new government programs and regulations that became the New Deal.

Chronology

1929, March 4: Herbert Hoover is inaugurated as President of the United States.

1929, September 3: Dow Jones Industrial Average reaches historic high of 381.

1929, October 29: Black Tuesday. The stock market drops as panic selling continues on record high volume.

1929, November 23: President Hoover requests that governors of the states expand public works projects to keep workers employed.

1930, June 17: President Hoover signs the Smoot-Hawley Tariff Act.

1930, September 9: The State Department begins to reduce immigration quotas until unemployment subsides.

1930, December 11: The Bank of the United States, with 60 branches in New York, closes its doors.

1931, September 20: Bank of England goes off the gold standard.

1931, October 7: Hoover proposes plan for the creation of the National Credit Corporation.

1932, February 2: The Reconstruction Finance Corporation

is created to lend billions to ailing businesses and banks.

1932, November 8: Franklin D. Roosevelt wins presidential election.

1933, January 30: Adolf Hitler becomes Chancellor of Germany.

1933, March 9: President Roosevelt begins legislative period where the New Deal is introduced.

1933, March 29: Congress passes bill establishing the Civilian Conservation Corps.

1933, April 19: President Roosevelt abandons the Gold Standard for the United States.

1934, January 2: The Dow Jones Industrial Average begins the year at 100.

1934, January 31: President Roosevelt returns the dollar to the gold standard at a new price of $35.00 per troy ounce.

1934, June 6: President Roosevelt signs the Securities and Exchange Act, which establishes the Securities and Exchange Commission.

1934, November 6: In mid-term elections, Democrats win two-thirds majority in Senate and make significant gains in the House.

1935, April 27: President Roosevelt signs a bill to create the Soil Conservation Service.

1935, May 6: President Roosevelt establishes Works Progress Administration (WPA).

1935, May: The Dow Jones Industrial Average begins a rally that will last until 1937.

1935, August 14: The Social Security Act becomes law. This law will provide pensions for Americans aged sixty-five and over.

1936, November 3: Franklin Roosevelt wins the presidential election by a landslide.

1937, April 12: The Supreme Court upholds the constitutionality of the national Labor Relations Act.

1937, August 2: Dow Jones Industrial Average begins a slide from 187 to end the year at 119.

1938, June 25: President Roosevelt signs the Fair Labor Standards Act (FLSA), which institutes a minimum wage and maximum working hours.

1939, May 22: Germany and Italy sign the Pact of Steel, which forms a military alliance between the two countries.

1939, July 1: President Roosevelt reorganizes the agencies created as part of the New Deal.

1939, September 1: Germany invades Poland. The nations of Europe begin to form alliances.

1940, May 10: Germany invades Luxembourg, the

Netherlands, and Belgium.

1940, June 22: France surrenders to Germany.

1940, November 5: Franklin Roosevelt wins third term as president.

Acknowledgments

I would like to thank Nadene Seiters and Lisa Zahn for their help in preparation of this book. The quotes are from the Brainy Quotes website. Unless otherwise noted, all the photographs are from the public domain.

Further Reading

Klein, Maury. *Rainbow's End – The Crash of 1929*. Oxford University Press, Inc. 2001.

Shales, Amity. *The Forgotten Man – A New History of the Great Depression*. Harper Perennial. 2008.

Watkins, T.H. *The Hungry Years – A Narrative History of the Great Depression in America*. Henry Holt and Company, LLC. 1999.

About the Author

Doug West is a retired engineer, small business owner, and experienced non-fiction writer with several books to his credit. His writing interests are general, with expertise in science, history, biographies, numismatics, and "How To" topics. Doug has a B.S. in Physics from the Missouri School of Science and Technology and a Ph.D. in General Engineering from Oklahoma State University. He lives with his wife and little dog, "Scrappy," near Kansas City, Missouri. Additional books by Doug West can be found at http://www.amazon.com/Doug-West/e/B00961PJ8M. Follow the author on Facebook at: https://www.facebook.com/30minutebooks.

Figure – Doug West (photo by Karina Cinnante)

Additional Books by Doug West

A Short Biography of the Scientist Sir Isaac Newton

A Short Biography of the Astronomer Edwin Hubble

Galileo Galilei – A Short Biography

Benjamin Franklin – A Short Biography

The American Revolutionary War – A Short History

Coinage of the United States – A Short History

John Adams – A Short Biography

In the Footsteps of Columbus (Annotated) Introduction and Biography Included (with Annie J. Cannon)

Alexander Hamilton – Illustrated and Annotated (with Charles A. Conant)

Harlow Shapley – Biography of an Astronomer

How to Write, Publish and Market Your Own Audio Book

Alexander Hamilton – A Short Biography

Index

R

Radio Corporation of America 36
Reconstruction Finance Corporation 17, 43
Roosevelt, Franklin D. ix, 25, 33, 44

S

Soil Conservation Service 29, 44
State Department 43
stock market vii, viii, 1, 2, 4, 5, 6, 8, 11, 14, 15, 43
Supreme Court 30, 45

U

United States vii, viii, 15, 16, 30, 33, 34, 36, 43, 44, 50

W

Wall Street Journal 8
Works Progress Administration 45
World War II ix, 30, 34, 38